ENDURANCE IN THE STORM

By

Charlie Anne Clemafry

Published by:

Table of Contents

Bliss is an enchanting feeling between loving yourself and being able to share it with others that will be happy about your progress

Hummorphosis

Exercise 1: Incoming! Spiritual attack! Spot the spiritual attack within the page. Ask yourself, how does this make me feel when I am reading this?

After the storm
And the sun showing its majestic radiance,
I feel a rainbow spread across my life;
My fears have disintegrated.
As I hold you and you hold me,
For once with a man, I feel free.
This hummingbird is morphing,
Becoming one with the chameleon.

Will the curse be broken?
From the beautiful creature that changes colour?
My feathers glisten from blue to green
And the lizard is wanting
To share his scales with me.

What is bird and what is lizard?
Confusion rudely invades my mind,
As scaly skin and feathers embrace.
He says, "I am yours, and you are mine."
This is when my head fills with doubt.
The hesitated "I love you!"
Was just the beginning of the cracks.

Hummorphosis: Part Two

Exercise 2: Incoming! Spiritual Attack! Spot the spiritual attack within the page. Ask yourself, how does this make me feel when I am reading this?

Colours of green and blue hue,
I thought I was living a fairy tale with you.
But this story didn't go that way, did it?
Not the one with the horse and the knight,
But this was the one where the guy got away.
This was the one where the woman
Was painted a villain.
Was it really that black and white?
Maybe I was just not cut out for this.
I wanted love,
But how deep was I willing to go?

Apparently not deep enough,
Because soul deep was too shallow for him.
He could not understand the pain I carried
From loving myself too much.

Maybe in the end, he was better off without me
Because the love we shared,
Was not meant to last eternally.
I now look back and see God's hand in it.
I can now see how He reached out many times,
But I snapped my jaws at His fingers
As He tried to calm me.

You would think this hummingbird
Would like to be led
Beside still waters and green pastures
But even the heavenliest lights
Could not hold my gaze
And at this point in my life,
God was no different…
Because the damage had already been done.

My feathers fell to the ground
As I screamed away my innocence.
I chose to cover myself
With fallen scales from the chameleon.
I had chased a fantasy and nothing more.
But my terrifying shriek was no longer lingering.
I was so angry with myself
That I couldn't make the leap.
The shriek that was meant to be a tweet…
Changed to a growl.

I thought, if I can't make it with a man,
Then how am I supposed to have a relationship
With a man I can't see?
Why couldn't I escape
The spiralling mess I had made?

Exercise 3: My current climb

TRIAL

Way through: How do I get through this trial when I feel I have no control in the struggle?

Prayer example: (have a go and write your own)

____

____

____

____

____

____

____

Hummorphosis: Part Three

The plan was ascension
And I hoped God would be patient with me.
I didn't realise the emptiness
That I was carrying
Until it had formed chains,
Anchored to my heart made of stone.
God breathed hope into my life
When I surrendered to the Holy Spirit
And my heart turned to flesh.
I was no longer numb
And the scales fell off.

God was patient enough to let time pass
And I grew back my wings.
I was no longer afraid
And I was transformed into an eagle.
I casted my cares
Onto the Lord's shoulders,
Like the lost lamb I was.
The chains of emptiness melted
And I was no longer lost and confused,
But found and loved.
I was ready and I raised a foot in the air,
Hanging off the cliff.
I closed my eyes…and I soared.

Exercise 4: Sprinkles of gold dust

Find the secret message of one of the book names of the bible. Find out what bible scripture this poem is inspired by. Hint: 40.

But those who trust **i**n the Lord will find new **s**trength. They will so**a**r h**i**gh on wings like e**a**gles. T**h**ey will run and not grow weary. They will walk and not faint.

Exercise 5: My current climb

<u>Trial</u>

Way through: How do I get through this trial when I feel I have no control in the struggle?

Prayer example: (have a go and write your own)

____

____

____

____

Hummorphosis: Part Four

Lord, You set my heart alight,
It is Your battle now that I want to fight.
The battle is won, this is true.
You have overcome the world
And I pray I could too.
But I have learnt, My first love,
That no matter how hard I strive,
Nothing can measure up to my strength…
When I lean on you.

No one has a more wonderful face,

You gave me free will, and you gave me grace.

The chains are now broken in Your name,

The hurt is now healing:

I will never be the same.

Exercise 6: My current climb

TRIAL

Way through: How do I get through this trial when I feel I have no control in the struggle?

Prayer example: (have a go and write your own)

____

____

____

____

____

____

____

Exercise 7: Cloudy no more

What piece of wisdom aligns with this poem based on how you feel?

The Next Step

Exercise 8: Incoming! Spiritual attack! Spot the spiritual attack within the page. Ask yourself, how does this make me feel when I am reading this?

I am petrified;
My best friend
Coming to an end
And my hands are tied.
Not against the bed
But mentally...
Oh, how I dread.
The reminder of an ex
A "friend" for all time,
Why do I feel this thought to be a crime?

I am terrified now of how it ends
And I can't play pretend.
I can't say it's alright
When at his mention, my skin grows tight.
Numbness spreads along me
And I know once I do this,
I can't go back
Or in my mind, I'll be off track.
I want this title,
I say it proudly,
But the echo of God's voice grows loudly.

My intro to love,
Twisted and cruel,
At my naked body, they drool.
I want you with no fear,
However with your "romance" and "adoration,"
You bring memories filled with tears.
I want to be happy and free.
I know this means not to flee.
I put my guard down, and they hurt me.

I will fight for Jesus and not you,
Who wipes my every tear as they trickle.
I love Holy Spirit's smile,
I adore Jesus' teachings and wit,
I have decided to not continue
With a guy like you though; I quit.
I know I'll always have Jesus by my side
Whereas you never rocked up for the ride.
The memory I battle is the past.
I love You, Jesus, with all my heart and mind.

Exercise 9: My current climb

<u>TRIAL</u>

Way through: How do I get through this trial when I feel I have no control in the struggle?

Prayer example: (have a go and write your own)

____

____

____

____

____

____

Exercise 10: Cloudy no more

What piece of wisdom aligns with this poem based on how you feel?

Eyes Open to Love

You are the most wonderful person
I have ever met
And You calm the raging fire
That is my heart.
When the fires are roaring,
Making my own life ablaze,
I love how You defuse each situation.
I will never know how You lift the smokey haze.
You hold the torch
To guide us through this unforgiving,
Cruel, merciless world
And I know
That You carry that burden alone.

Sometimes it takes more than two to stay true,
To what we were made to be and do.
I am happy
That You will return soon.
Love surrounds You,
So never forget.
You are the light in the darkness,
The way maker and the miracle worker.
You are every bit capable,
Even when it seems impossible.
You are enough to me just as you are.

You don't need fancy degrees
Or an expensive car.
You have taught me a new definition of success:
Strength, endurance, courage and hope
And so many other qualities I could confess.
I love you, Jesus
And You have made sacrifices
I can't even comprehend.
There's no more beating around the bush
Or trading in being happy over being right.

I love You, and when You arrive back on Earth,
I just want to hold you tight.
I love it when You have ideas and help me,
Holy Spirit.
So I will love You forever
Until the end of eternity.
You fill me with joy and peace
Because I trust in You.
I overflow with confident hope now;
This is true.

Exercise 11: Sprinkles of gold dust

Find the secret message in one of the book names of the bible. Find out which Bible scripture this poem is inspired by. Hint: Number 15.

I p**r**ay that G**o**d, the source of hope, will fill you co**m**pletely with joy and pe**a**ce because you trust i**n** him. Then you will overflow with confident hope through the power of the Holy **S**pirit.

Exercise 12: My current climb

TRIAL

Way through: how do I get through this trial when I feel I have no control in the struggle?

Prayer example: (have a go and write your own)

____

____

____

____

____

____

Healing From Infection

Exercise 13: incoming! Spiritual attack! Spot the spiritual attack within the page. Ask yourself, how does this make me feel when I am reading this?

I felt trapped by addiction,
Like the liquid confidence
That I wanted more than joy.
Each shot inflating my false charisma,
As much it was another blow to my self-esteem.
He corrupted me, and I didn't even know.
I was blinded by his charm because I loved…
That suave guy called Alcohol.

All of the many delusional combinations I had
Were to prove my love to him…
But he poisoned me.
I thought he could take care of me,
But he left me with a dried-up heart.
I thought he loved me back,
But he left me on the curb with a desperate plea
To figure out where the heck I am.

That suave guy called Alcohol walked away
And the same adrenaline rush
To beat the town drunk
Was just not the same.
I traded in my love for something stronger,
Because the hole that was eating away at me
Was not getting any smaller.

Healing From Infection: Part Two

Exercise 14: Incoming! Spiritual Attack! Spot the spiritual attack within the page. Ask yourself, how does this make me feel when I am reading this?

Greeny held me with the promises of the world...
But soon after, I was fooled.
I saw the colours of the buds on the table
And after a while, they appeared to be dark.
I denied he was bad for me as I was for him.
In the end,
I moved onto the only relationship I could keep:
Anything stronger than what I had already tried.

I got hurt in the process,
More times than I could count.
I missed Alcohol
And eventually wandered
Back to familiar habits.
Me clinging to the words he fed me
And him encouraging me…
Made our love infected.
I'm setting fire to the memories
That I couldn't process at the time.

I'm lighting the match
And dropping it onto the firewood now.
My traumas can no longer hide
In the crevices of my mind.
I'm sweeping away the demons,
Like the ashes of my past existence.
These once tormented me,
But I am healing now.

I am on my way to recovery.
I am relieved
That the images are burning to a cinder.
You are out of my life
And I am grateful to be sober.
I'm sober because of you, Jesus.
I thank You for everything good
That has ever happened in my life
And everything good to come.

Exercise 15: My current climb

TRIAL

Way through: How do I get through this trial when I feel I have no control in the struggle?

Prayer example: (have a go and write your own)

____

____

____

____

____

____

Exercise 16: Cloudy no more

What piece of wisdom aligns with this poem based on how you feel?

Why I Love You

All praise to God,
The father of our Lord Jesus Christ.
At the thought of You,
The below will be all true;
About how much I love You.
Holy Spirit, Jesus and Heavenly Father.
You are trustworthy and compassionate,
Faithful and filled to the brim with grace.
All of my worst chapters are now less confusing
Because You are in the thick of the ink.

I now realise that my book of life can be exciting
Just by focusing on what is right in front of me
And making the most of it.
I may not be able to delete my past,
But You accept me wholeheartedly.
You hauled me over Your shoulders
When I was drenched in the mud and smelt.
You push me to be the best version of me,
Through trials of fire, You test me.

So that's why I wrote You a poem.
I have loved you for so long.
You are genuine and loving,
You're dependable, sweet, caring
And forever daring to battle my blues away.
My storm clouds have no chance
When You are on their case.
Loving you is the best part of my day.
Reading the bible with you now is like play.

Exercise 17: Sprinkles of gold dust

Find the secret message in one of the book names of the bible. Find out which Bible scripture this poem is inspired by. Hint: this number appears twice in the scripture.

All **p**raise to God, th**e** Father of our Lord Jesus Chris**t**. It is by his great m**e**rcy that we have been born again, because God raised Jesus Christ f**r**om the dead. Now we live with great expectation.

Exercise 18: My current climb

TRIAL

Way through: How do I get through this trial when I feel I have no control in the struggle?

Prayer example: (have a go and write your own)

____

____

____

____

____

This is what I live for

Why is this so hard to write?
I know the page won't bite.
I guess what I'm trying to say
Is You bring my soul alight.
Like a jigsaw puzzle of a thousand pieces,
Looking closely, we are so much more complex
And I don't want us to come apart.
We click together so perfectly
And I'm grateful that You put me back together.

My heart melted like butter in Your presence,
A puddle of shyness, and that's when I stutter:
I-I love you too.
Especially when I feel grey, black or blue.
I'm here to handle the projects we do together.
Thank You, Holy Spirit and Heavenly Father!
Any problem that I struggle to face in my life,
I know You'll be there,
Whether it be emotional, physical,
Spiritual or mental.

There is so many more adventures to come!
With You, I feel like I'm always at the arcade.
I will take Your hand in faith
Again and again.
Flashing lights illuminate your face just right.
You lift me high as I worship Your name,
Jesus, You bring me up to the heights
of Mount Zion.

I am stronger than I think
Because you encouraged me in this festive rink.
I want to be linking arms
With You every second of every day,
When You arrive,
I'll be holding a banner and beg You to stay.
Knowing Your presence
Makes the internal tsunami subside.
As You listen to me babble,
My love eternally thrives.
This is what I live for.

Exercise 19: My current climb

TRIAL

Way through: How do I get through this trial when I feel I have no control in the struggle?

Prayer example: (have a go and write your own)

____

____

____

____

Exercise 20: Cloudy no more

What piece of wisdom aligns with this poem based on how you feel?

No More Pretend

You're in my heart
And You make me feel
Like I'm no longer shopping at a mart.
No more swiping to find a match.
You are such a catch! I…you know,
I just want to go with the flow
And You want me to know
I am cherished by You.
I want to cry with joy
And I don't mean to pry,
But I'm curious what You're up to, my Jesus.

Even though my head right now is like
Breakfast at the zoo,
I want nothing more to do with them
And everything more to do with you.
The frustration I carry for humans
Does not apply to you.
It just proves you are perfect for me.

I put away the figments of my imagination
Just so I can hang out with you.
In the simplicity, somehow…
You make reality feel more enjoyable.
You make everything that I used to find dull,
Brand new, and I see life in a whole new light.
Being with You is a realistic dream come true.

Shade and Light

I'll be the shade if You be my light.
As You reflect off my soul, I become the night.
You walk Your days burning bright.
As long as You stay a moment, I'll be alright.
I'm on a carousel that's taking flight.
My desire is like a flood of light.
I cannot seem to clearly express my love.
Meet me in my dreams this quaking night.

Be mine until the morning light
And I promise that I'll hold you tight.
This is what I'm hopin'
And this is what I've chosen.
I want to be Your faithful servant.
You love me as I am, and I enjoy Your company
And that's enough for me.
I'll savour that time when You're not busy.
I'll pray on a star You come back home safely.
This is what I'm hopin'
And this is what I've chosen.

Exercise 21: Sprinkles of gold dust

Find the secret message in one of the book names of the bible. Find out which Bible scripture this poem is inspired by. Hint: number 1.

I pray that your h**e**arts will be flooded with light so that you can understand the confident ho**pe** **he** ha**s** g**i**ven to those he c**a**lled-his holy people who are his rich a**n**d glorious inheritance.

Her Tribe

In a jungle where love was scarce,
A faint roaring could be heard.
The sun arose, and the pride awakened.
The pride of lions
Had sons and daughters of all shapes and sizes.
All of them were lions and lionesses:
All except one of the members of the pride.
She had a face, body and tail like her pride,
But she was stripy, and they were not.
She tried to roar like the others,
But instead, she chuffed.
Her pride tried to teach her lion things,
But she always did it the wrong way.
In the reflection of a river,
She scowled at herself with frustration.

With a mighty thrash,
She splashed her watery reflection.
She wanted to see a proud lion,
But instead, she saw a stripy outcast.
She thought about fleeing
From a fate she could not control.
But she was determined to find her tribe.
She tried to hop about with the antelope,
But she scared them away.
She tried to fly like an eagle,
But found out she could not fly,
No matter how hard she tried.
She could run with a cheetah,
But she ran out of puff.

She tried to stretch her neck out
To eat leaves like a giraffe,
But she was not tall enough
And her neck could not stretch very far at all.
She ran back to the river,
Battling with her reflection.
A puffed-out, sweaty, dirty stranger
Stared back at her,
But this time, there was another next to her.
She scanned this creature that looked like her.
Could it be?
It had a face, a body and a tail like her.
It was stripy like her.

She chuffed at the creature
And it chuffed back.
She smiled a big, toothy grin
And he smiled back.
It was her tribe!
The girl tiger thought she would be too different,
But her orange and black stripes did not seem
To bother the white and black tiger.
Soon enough, the two of them
Started hanging out.
The tigers were the same age and dated.
The girl tiger started to become proud
Of having stripes and, in general, being a tiger.
She was no longer alone
And because this male tiger believed in her,
She started to believe in herself, too.

She had fallen in love with herself
Because she had met someone like her.
She saw how amazing life was when
She accepted herself
And because she loved herself,
She loved her new partner in her life.
To him, she did not need to be
Like any of the other animals.
She just needed to be her tigery self.

Exercise 22: My current climb

TRIAL

Way through: How do I get through this trial when I feel I have no control in the struggle?

Prayer example: (have a go and write your own)

____

____

____

____

____

____

My Love for You

I was lost in an oasis.
I thought I'd just stay in homeostasis.
The fear of overthinking; oh, how I felt
I was sinking.
The start of our chapters together
Have been progressing in length.
We seem to be making it work,
Each chapter better than the next.
A relationship with you expands beyond
Input/output chemical reactions.

ENDURANCE IN THE STORM

I've held onto our budding mutual love,
Because of the fun, laughter
And good times we share.
Our love has seemed to erupt!
I thought with my big emotions
That you'd leave without a doubt,
But you haven't, and I applaud that.
Thank you, my Jesus, for calming me
And being there when most would walk
Like so many have…

Exercise 23: Cloudy no more

What piece of wisdom aligns with this poem based on how you feel?

My Love for You: Part Two

I'm glad you are the last man standing
After everything that went on in my past.
I'm more confident to take charge of my life
Now that God has united us.
I am hopeful about our future together
And I am moving towards being humbler,
Like a nephilim transformed to a sheep.
There were days I was reckless and unruly
But now I'm bouncing off God to be loyal,
Whilst also celebrating my womanhood.

Although I'm following a new path,
One of creativity and spark,
I still remember my life when it was in the dark.
Jesus, You were one of the only beings
That pulled me out of my mind's oozy tar
And this time I plan to stay unstuck.
I was wandering in circles,
Like being stuck in a game with no instructions.
I thought I could win on my own,
But I was wrong by far.

I needed Holy Spirit to guide me
And have faith
That the sun would rise the next day,
Regardless of the day I've had.
You remind me of that
Just by being You, my God!
There's nothing we can't do.
Jesus uniting us, my darling, has given me hope
To believe in love.
I love you, and loving you is how I will stay.

My Little Sunshine

You are my sunshine,
I am yours and you are mine.
Always know throughout this time,
Oh, how I'm…
Missing you dearly.
That Thursday
You were ripped from me spiritually,
But you were also away from harm.
I love you with all my heart
And even at this moment
My tongue is griefly tart.

I'll see you again.
I just don't know when.
I have hope as much as a new day,
That one day, for real, you will stay.
I love you, my sweet little man.
I will do everything I can
So you are happy, healthy and safe.
I cannot reunite with you the way I want,
So into my mind I go,
To avoid the terrors of the outside world
That haunt me day and night.

As long as we have faith,
We will see each other again,
Unsupervised and safe.
I believe that one day we will.
I am going to learn to discover a better way,
So that you can have your best chance.
I am going to continue to pray
That they protect you long term.
That's my stance on this unthinkable scenario.

I am fearful as much as I have hope,
But in order to stay on an even slope,
I need to be a better person:
Hence why my prayers
Are mixed with big emotions.
I cannot provide for you
As I cannot keep going down this road.

Never forget I love you always,
No ifs and no buts:
That will never change.
By your free will, if you so choose,
I will help guide you
To be the best version of yourself.
I was not at my best when I birthed you,
But with what I had,
I did my best, and since having you,
My faith for what I believe in
Has been put to the ultimate test.

Exercise 24: My current climb

TRIAL

Way through: How do I get through this trial when I feel I have no control in the struggle?

Prayer example: (have a go and write your own)

____

____

____

____

____

____

Out of XP

And just like that,
There's blackness, and that's that.
Spawning rate is low
Because the guy I fell for is always on the go.
Trying to recharge,
But even all of my alliances
Cannot fill the emptiness in my heart.
There is an aching that he is gone.
The intensity of a gamer gone dark.

I can't get you out of my head,
The flashes of light fading;
That the connection of where he is…is dead.
But just like how Jesus raised up Lazarus,
I do not give up on him.
I look to the Lord for help, and I pray.
I wait confidently for God to save him
I believe my God will certainly hear me.
Just like that,
When I thought you were gone for good
And I was lost in disarray;
Your light flashed up.

I sprang to the keyboard; I typed oh so fast.
Nothing could stop my fingers from typing,
Losing in my mind the time that had passed.
You're alive!
You're safe.
You're gaining it all back
And my mind is refocusing.
I'm getting back on track.

The love I have for you,
I can't explain it,
But I'd trade in my PC,
If that's what you asked of me.
With my love for you,
I can cross to the darkest realms
And believe I'll return.
It may be just a game,
But I love my Jesus all the same.

Exercise 25: Sprinkles of gold dust

Find the secret message in one of the book names of the bible. Find out which Bible scripture this poem is inspired by. Hint: number 7.

As for **me**, I look to the Lord for help. I wa**i**t **c**onfidently for God to s**a**ve me, and my God will certainly **h**ear me.

In Bed by Ten

He wants to be in bed by ten,
Would I just be able to start again?
His hands feel like heaven.
Touching me as if I'll disappear,
Loving me wholly is what I fear.
To love again like I did so fully,
To be his lover and not appear to be a bully.
To uplift him in times of struggle,
To lose it all to him and
Gain his love forevermore.

When the chips are down, I pitch in.
When the weather is upon frowned,
He ditches everything.
Can I do the same?
To keep up with the ever-growing love?
Can I be that girl of his dreams
And ignore what destiny has planned for me?

I love him so. I wish I could properly show
That through it all I will stay.
This is how I show love;
Nothing or all the way.
No need to trust in money,
But to trust in our loving God.

Exercise 26: Cloudy no more

What piece of wisdom aligns with this poem based on how you feel?

Exercise 27: Sprinkles of gold dust

Find the secret message in one of the book names of the bible. Find out which Bible scripture this poem is inspired by. Hint: number 6.

Teach **t**hose who are **ri**ch in this world not to be proud and not to trust in their **m**oney, which is s**o** unreliable. Their **t**rust s**h**ould be in God, who richl**y** gives us all we need for our enjoyment.

Exercise 28: My current climb

TRIAL

Way through: How do I get through this trial when I feel I have no control in the struggle?

Prayer example: (have a go and write your own)

____

____

____

____

____

____

Rendering My Love

There's a reason these people
Keep coming back to my attention.
These people that seem to be glimmers
In the speck of my life.
One moment, they are here.
The next they are gone.
Like ghosts, floating through the haze.
Oh, I wish I could erase.
But they stay.

They are not going anywhere.

Just because I block,

Does not mean their existence stops.

I'm not in control.

They move on,

Because I'm not their be-all/end-all.

I'm just a person, and so are they.

I surrender them all to God;

They'll make someone happy one day.

Perhaps they even already have,
Just not in the way I understand.
Letting them go was easier
With my Heavenly Helper,
But remembering the good
And leaving it at that,
Now that's the real obstacle,
Like the eating of the fat.

You're guilty to indulge,
Because without salt it tastes of nothing.
You could not believe someone to love you,
When you are so snappy.
But they did, and he does
And you can love yourself, too.

It's alright to tuck your own self in at night.
It's okay to not be perfect every day.
It's safe because you're surrounded
By those that protect and love you.
You walk and talk as yourself
And let the rest shine through.

Roses Are Pink

Roses are red,
But can also be pink, yellow and white.
They may have sharp thorns,
But people still love them,
Regardless of their nip and bite.
They smell so sweet,
Enough at least for perfumes,
Soaps and hand creams.
They are the reason poems like these
Are made for love that is true.

If love was easy,
They wouldn't need roses
To depict what love is.
It isn't always sweet like honey.
Sometimes love that is so strong…
Is sharp, blunt and thorny.
Sometimes the bond is so intense,
That we need to use our agency.

Sometimes love sucks
Like having hopes of something
Amazing coming in the mail…
But it does not come
And you feel your happy feelings set sail.

Sometimes love is exciting and pure,
Genuine and trustworthy…
But for balance to coexist,
We must appreciate this.
Love is not consistently happy clappy,
But it is those moments
That you weigh up
If it is worth it to pursue.

Exercise 29: Cloudy no more

What piece of wisdom aligns with this poem based on how you feel?

Roses Are Pink: Part Two

Maybe the reason the rose is still in your life

Is to teach you something.

Something that you don't want to know,

But is necessary to advance to the next chapter For you to be a better person.

Maybe that reason is to let go

And love that person

Because the bitterness welling up inside you

Just isn't worth it.

I don't know much about love.

But I do know it is never
In the package you plan.
If you didn't get hurt from crushes,
Maybe you wouldn't have gotten so hungry
For peace and contentment?
If you didn't get betrayed
By those closest to you,
What would there be to test your bond?
Is it worth it to wither and die,
Thornless and arranged into a bouquet?

Sometimes when you drop the expectations,
You find love.
Maybe it's awkward to be genuine
Because you leave yourself open to rejection.
But maybe that's what love is.
You taking that chance,
With someone who has proved
They would conquer your heart
In any way you ask.

If it isn't from a place of love,

Then is it worth it at all?

Without love, I am just a noisy gong

And clanging cymbal!

Love does not have to make sense,

Like the rose does not always have to have its Thorns clipped to be admired by its beauty.

Love is the cure to all disease.

The roses know this,

So why don't I?

Maybe the answer is answerless.

Maybe I can't put it in a bottle like I thought.
Maybe the reason I still love
After everything I have been through is…
I just do.
Maybe climbing the narrow path
Is trudging through with love anyway
And enduring the storms
When they come out of nowhere.

Maybe it's about having a giggle
With a loved one
You have freshly reunited with,
Even when kindness seems childish.
Can I give up every confusing memory I cling to
That solves the question of who I am?
Love is everything I can't explain…

Maybe the answer is I don't know what love is
And maybe the way forward is to be okay with The unknown
And to surrender it to the Good Shepherd,
To be grateful for another day on Earth
And hopefully one day raise
And keep a child at birth.

www.ingramcontent.com/pod-product-compliance
Lightning Source LLC
LaVergne TN
LVHW020048110826
045133LV00029B/680

* 9 7 8 1 9 2 3 6 5 5 9 5 9 *